Science at the Edge

Body Sculpting

D0279031

Sally Morgan

Heinemann
LIBRARY

www.heinemann.co.uk/library
Visit our website to find out more information about **Heinemann Library** books.

To order:
☎ Phone 44 (0) 1865 888066
🖷 Send a fax to 44 (0) 1865 314091
💻 Visit the Heinemann Bookshop at www.heinemann.co.uk/library to browse our catalogue and order online.

First published in Great Britain by Heinemann Library, Halley Court, Jordan Hill, Oxford OX2 8EJ, part of Harcourt Education. Heinemann is a registered trademark of Harcourt Education Ltd.

Editorial: Lucy Thunder and Harriet Milles
Design: Joanna Malivoire and Celia Jones
Illustrations: Nick Hawken
Picture Research: Melissa Allison and Liz Savery
Production: Camilla Smith

Originated by Repro Multi Warna
Printed and bound in China by South China Printing

The paper used to print this book comes from sustainable resources.

ISBN 0 431 14907 0 (hardback)
09 08 07 06 05
10 9 8 7 6 5 4 3 2 1

ISBN 0 431 14912 7 (paperback)
10 09 08 07 06
10 9 8 7 6 5 4 3 2 1

British Library Cataloguing in Publication Data
Morgan, Sally
Body sculpting. – (Science at the Edge)
646.7'5
A full catalogue record for this book is available from the British Library.

Acknowledgements
The Publishers would like to thank the following for permission to reproduce photographs: American Society of Plastic Surgeons p24; Corbis (Gregory Pace) p45, (Jeffrey L Rotman) p28, (Jose Luis Pelaez Inc) p39, (Kevin R Morris) p6; Corbis Saba/Najlah Feanny p22; Corbis Sygma pp31, 50, (Bob Collier Photos) p20, (Patrick Robert) p37; Getty Images (Stone) p8; Harcourt Education Ltd (Nick Hawken) p26; Mediscan p19; PA Photos p9; Reuters (Gary Hershorn) p40; Rex Features (Woman's Own) p47; Science Photo Library p51, (Victor Habbick Visions) p57, (W Industries/James King-Holmes) p54, (BSIP, LA/Caby Valence) p48, (Coneyl Jay) pp32, 36, (Custom Medical Stock Photo) p33, (Custom Medical Stock Photo/M Marshall) p43, (Custom Medical Stock Photo/Michael English) p11, (Dr P Marazzi) p18, (John MacFarland) p10, (Lauren Shear) p34, (Mauro Fermariello) p13, (Michelle Del Guercio) pp14, 42, (MIT AI Lab/Surgical Planning Lab/Brigham & Women's Hospital) p53, (Pascal Goetgheluck) pp15, 29; Topham Picturepoint p5; Wellcome Trust pp17, 46.

Cover photograph of cosmetic eyelid surgery reproduced with permission of Science Photo Library (Coneyl Jay).

The Publishers would like to thank Mr V Ilankovan, Consultant Maxillofacial Surgeon, for his assistance in the preparation of this book.

Every effort has been made to contact copyright holders of any material reproduced in this book. Any omissions will be rectified in subsequent printings if notice is given to the Publishers.

Disclaimer
All the Internet addresses (URLs) given in this book were valid at the time of going to press. However, due to the dynamic nature of the Internet, some addresses may have changed, or sites may have changed or ceased to exist since publication. While the author and the Publishers regret any inconvenience this may cause readers, no responsibility for any such changes can be accepted by either the author or the Publishers.

Contents

Any words appearing in the text in bold,
like this, are explained in the Glossary.

Introduction

In 1992 Louise Ashby was 22 years old, and dreamed of an acting career in Hollywood. One night, as she and a friend were driving home, another car crashed into them. Louise was seriously injured, and the left side of her face was virtually destroyed.

A few decades earlier, Louise would have had to learn to live with her disfigured face. But over a period of ten years her appearance was gradually restored to normal, thanks to advances in the field of plastic surgery.

Plastic surgery

The word 'plastic' in plastic surgery does not refer to using plastic materials. Another meaning of the word plastic is 'capable of being moulded or of receiving form', and this is what is meant in plastic surgery. Plastic surgery involves processes such as moving skin and **tissue** from one part of the body to another, stretching things out and reshaping them.

There are two uses for plastic surgery – reconstructive surgery and cosmetic surgery. Reconstructive surgery is carried out in order to restore a more normal appearance to abnormal or injured parts of the body, as in the case of Louise Ashby. The repair of wounds and fractures of the facial bones are common procedures in plastic surgery. Other examples include the removal of skin **cancers**, repair of **genetic** defects and repairing skin damage caused by burns.

Cosmetic surgery is performed to enhance the appearance rather than to correct injuries or abnormalities. Common kinds of cosmetic surgery include **facelifts**, nose reshaping, and removal of fat. In recent years there has been a great upsurge in the popularity of cosmetic surgery in richer countries, particularly in the USA. In 2002, nearly 7 million cosmetic procedures (both surgical and non surgical) were performed in the USA, more than three times the number in 1997. Over 80 per cent of those who had cosmetic surgery were women, although the number of men has risen rapidly in recent years.

During the Falklands War in 1982, British soldier Simon Weston suffered burns to almost half his body. Since then he has undergone over 75 painful operations to repair the damage. Simon's life is an example of personal courage and triumph over suffering. Despite his severe injuries, he undertakes endless charitable work. In 1992 he was awarded the OBE.

Cosmetic concerns

Plastic surgery raises many issues. As advances in technology mean that more procedures can be carried out more readily, there are increasingly difficult questions to consider. What happens when cosmetic surgery goes wrong? Should young people have cosmetic surgery? Is it ethical for doctors to completely change the appearance of their patient? In this book you can read about plastic surgery, and learn more about these issues. You can learn about the techniques used by surgeons and the science behind the technology. Find out also how technologies such as cloning, brain **transplants** and **virtual reality** may shape the future of plastic surgery. Decide for yourself whether cosmetic surgery is a good or bad thing.

The rise of plastic surgery

Reconstructive surgery was probably first used in India in approximately 600 BC, when doctors used skin from the forehead to rebuild the noses of people who had had them cut off as a punishment. However, it was not until the development of **anaesthesia**, towards the end of the 19th century, that the first real advances in plastic surgery took place.

There were further major developments during World War I. Thousands of soldiers were badly wounded on the battlefield. Never before had such large numbers of soldiers been so severely injured. Doctors, such as the French army surgeon Hippolyte Morestin, had to learn how to deal with severe facial injuries, burns and lost limbs. It was from these first experiences of reconstructive surgery that surgeons developed techniques for plastic surgery on the nose and the face. Advances in reconstructive surgery were also made during World War II.

During the 1950s implants to enlarge breasts were used for the first time, and **liposuction** (the removal of fat) was developed in the 1970s. Since then plastic surgery has developed rapidly, mainly because of advances in equipment – for example, the development of **endoscopes** and **laser** surgery.

What is beautiful?

Many people have cosmetic surgery in order to make themselves more beautiful. But what is considered beautiful in one society can be considered completely unattractive and undesirable in another.

Fat is often thought to indicate that a person is healthy and well-off. In many parts of West Africa, a full body is considered highly desirable and linked to fertility. In some cultures young women planning to get married eat heavily before their wedding in order to put on as much weight as possible. In fact, there is medical evidence to suggest that women who have fat around their hips and less on their waist are less likely to suffer from infertility problems.

In modern Western society, a slim woman is considered beautiful and many women will undergo cosmetic surgery to reduce the fat on their hips and buttocks.

'Until I came to America, I never knew thin was beautiful.'
Young male exchange student from the Ivory Coast

In many cultures, exaggerated features such as extra-large ear lobes, big lips, long necks or tiny feet are considered to increase the attractiveness of women. For instance, some Senegalese women increase the natural thickness of their upper lip by pricking it repeatedly until it is permanently inflamed and swollen.

In the Karen Padaung tribe of Burma, a long neck is considered beautiful. When a girl reaches the age of five, she is given her first neck ring and as she gets older, new ones are added. The rings stretch her neck until it is about 30 cm long. In some areas the Karen Padaung put large pieces of ivory in their ear lobes instead of wearing neck rings.

Lotus Feet

One of the more extreme examples of altering parts of the body is the ancient Chinese custom of foot binding. Tiny feet, called lotus feet, were considered a sign of beauty and attractiveness in women. Young girls from wealthy families would have their feet bound when they were about five years old. Their toes were bent under and bones were broken to force the front and back of the foot together. At the end of this binding process the young girls had feet about ten centimetres long. However, these tiny feet meant that the girl could only shuffle around and often had to be carried.

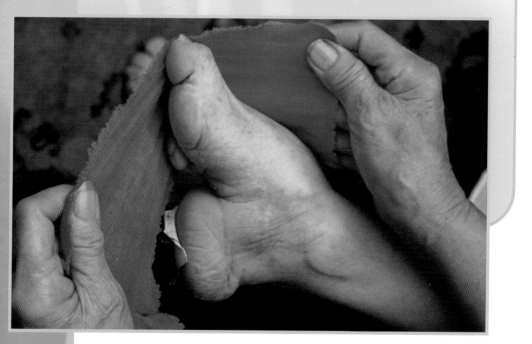

Media pressure

Today the idea that it is desirable to be young and slim is reinforced everywhere we look. 'Perfect' faces and bodies appear on magazine covers and TV screens and stare down from advertizing hoardings. It is not surprising that young people today worry about their appearance, and older men and woman try to look younger.

However, what we see in photos and on films can be an illusion. Faces are often retouched to remove the slightest spot, blemish or wrinkle. Sometimes photos are stretched to make a person looks taller and thinner. In films, star actors often have a 'body double' – someone with a fit, well-muscled body who stands in for the actor in some shots.

In an attempt to live up to these ideals, more people than ever are undergoing plastic surgery, especially cosmetic surgery. Traditionally it is women who opt for cosmetic surgery, but the numbers of men having cosmetic procedures is growing fast. They now make up about 20 per cent of plastic surgery patients, double the percentage of fifteen years ago.

Risky business

All surgery is risky, and plastic surgery is no different. Reconstructive procedures can be long and complex, and things can go wrong. Patients are made aware of the risks, but for them the benefits of a normal appearance far outweigh any risk.

Cosmetic surgery is different. Patients choose to have surgery in order to improve their appearance – so is the risk worth it? Not surprisingly, patients are very unhappy when things go wrong and they end up with a disfigured face or a scarred body. They may need to have further operations to correct the mistakes of the first one.

The American actress and singer, Cher, makes no secret of the fact that she has had cosmetic surgery - but is it worth the risk?

The problems caused by mistakes in plastic surgery are not just physical. Patients can suffer emotionally and psychologically as well. Often the victims of mistakes feel guilty or think that they are being punished for vanity. As cosmetic surgery increases in popularity, awareness of the risks becomes more important.

The plastic surgeon's toolbox

In recent decades plastic surgery has changed out of all recognition. Today's surgeons can suck fat out of the body, move **tissues** from one area to another, and rebuild damaged parts using bone and muscle from elsewhere. In order to carry out these complex operations, surgeons need specialist equipment and techniques. This chapter takes a closer look at the plastic surgeon's toolbox.

Endoscopy

The **endoscope** is an instrument that allows a surgeon to look inside the body without opening it up. It consists of a snake-like tube containing **optical fibres** connected to a tiny camera and a bright light. The tube is inserted through a small incision (cut) and manipulated until the end reaches the site where the surgeon wants to operate. The optical fibres send images from the surgical site to a tiny camera. The images are magnified on a viewing screen, allowing the surgeon to view the surgical site almost as clearly as if the body had been cut open.

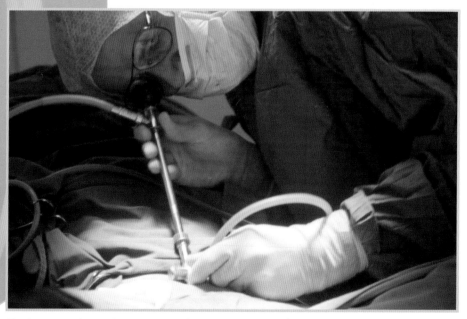

During an endoscopic operation, the surgeon views the operation using a video camera attached to a tube carrying optical fibres, which is inserted into the body. Surgical instruments are also inserted down one or more other tubes.

Endoscopes can also be used to carry out operations. To do this, tiny surgical instruments such as **scalpels** or forceps are inserted down another tube through another small incision. The surgeon uses the endoscope to watch what he is doing at the surgical site.

There are several advantages to doing endoscopic operations. Instead of the large incision needed in a conventional operation, only a few small incisions, each less than a couple of centimetres long, are needed to insert the endoscope probe and other instruments. This means that there is less likelihood of nerve damage, less bleeding and swelling and patients recover more quickly. An endoscopic breast reconstruction, for instance (see pages 22–3) can be carried out with just three or four short incisions.

> 'You are looking at a flat TV monitor, and operating a very thin instrument through very small holes in the tummy. So even just appreciating that and working in a three-dimensional space is very difficult.'
>
> Abdominal surgeon, Dr Nick Taffinder

Microsurgery

Microsurgery has allowed plastic surgeons to carry out incredibly delicate operations in which tiny blood vessels and nerves are rejoined. Before the advent of microsurgery, if you had a severed finger or a big open wound on your body, there was little that could be done. Today it is likely that the surgeon can rejoin the finger or take tissues from other parts of the body to repair an open wound.

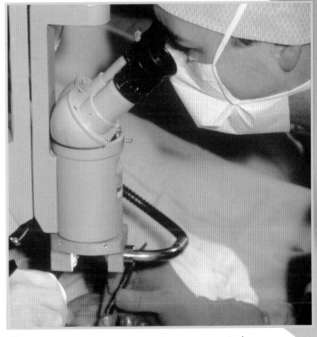

During microsurgery, operations are carried out while viewing through the microscope. The needles and sutures used to stitch up wounds have to be small so that they do not damage blood vessels and nerves.

Tissue flaps

One common procedure in reconstructive surgery is the removal of a piece of skin, muscle and blood vessels from one part of the body for use in rebuilding another part. Such pieces of tissue are called **flaps**.

Tissues receive blood through tiny blood vessels called capillaries. The blood brings oxygen and nutrients to the tissue **cells**. When tissues are moved, the surgeon has to ensure that the cells have a blood supply, otherwise they will starve of oxygen and die. A tissue flap will also usually contain some nerves, and these have to be reconnected so that the patient has feeling in the part of the body being rebuilt.

Sometimes a surgeon removes the blood vessels along with the tissues and then reconnects them when the tissue has been moved. The surgeon may even include large blood vessels in the tissue flap. Alternatively a tissue flap can be removed without a blood supply and then connected up to local blood vessels in its new position.

Under normal conditions a blood vessel that is cut or damaged will constrict (close up) to cut off the flow of blood. But blood vessels in a tissue flap have to be kept open at all times so that they can be joined up in their new location. Surgeons keep the blood vessels open during tissue **transplants** by using a drug that stops the normal constriction response.

> 'When I first started there were no **sutures**, no needles, and no instruments small enough for surgery of this type. I used to make the needles myself under the microscope, and we borrowed or copied jewellers' instruments. A big breakthrough came from the **Silicon Valley** and its microassembly techniques. Engineers were able to make needles for me that were thinner than your hair and drill the needle eye with a **laser**.'
>
> Dr Harry Bunke, pioneer in the field of microsurgery

Lasers

The laser is another important piece of equipment for the plastic surgeon. A laser produces a very intense beam of light of one **wavelength** (light of one colour of the spectrum). A beam of laser light concentrates a large quantity of energy into a small space, making the laser a very powerful instrument.

Lasers are widely used in plastic surgery. The laser cuts through the skin like an ultra-fine scalpel. Its heat seals the blood vessels in the instant that they are cut so there is little bleeding. The finely focused beam of light improves the precision of the surgeon.

A new trend in laser surgery is to use the special properties of different wavelengths of laser light to treat a range of problems. For example, red birthmarks known as 'port wine stains' can be treated using yellow laser light, which is more strongly absorbed by the red port wine stain than by other tissues. This means the birthmark can be destroyed without affecting the skin cells around it.

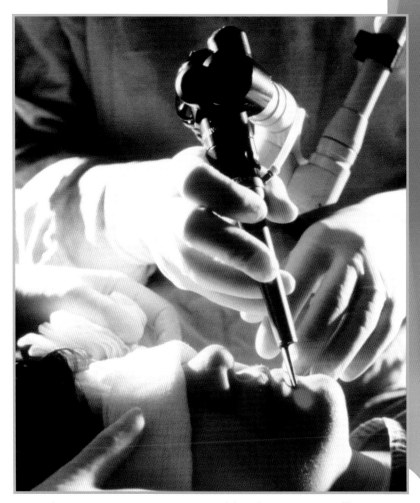

Lasers are an important new tool for plastic surgeons. They can be aimed down blood vessels or sent down optical fibres in endoscopes to reach areas that are otherwise inaccessible. Here the laser is removing a mark on the skin.

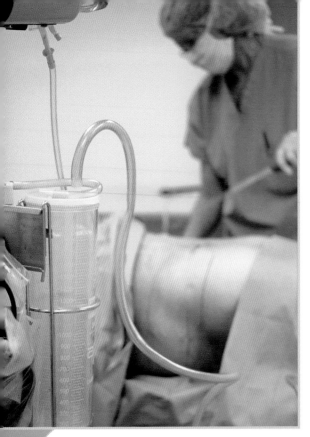

Liposuction

A popular cosmetic procedure is **liposuction**, a technique for removing fat to reshape the body. Before liposuction was developed in the 1970s, fat deposits were removed by cutting them out with a scalpel, which often gave uneven results and caused heavy bleeding. Today the surgeon injects the fatty area with a large quantity of anaesthetic liquid that deadens the pain and causes the pockets of fat to become firm and swollen. A thin tube is inserted into the area and a vacuum pump sucks out unwanted fat.

Liposuction is the most common cosmetic surgery in the USA. Nearly 373,000 procedures were performed in 2002. However, liposuction is not a substitute for diet and exercise, nor is it a cure for **cellulite** (the dimpled skin often found on the thighs, buttocks and abdomen).

Liposuction is a popular procedure used to remove fat from areas such as the stomach, hips and thighs. As the name suggests, fat is literally sucked out of the body.

Collagen implants

Collagen is a **protein** found in the skin, where it helps to give the skin its elasticity and support. As the skin ages, collagen is broken down or damaged and the skin becomes wrinkled. Doctors have found that it is safe to inject collagen and similar substances into the skin without them being rejected by the body.

Collagen can be used to remove wrinkles, but also to enhance the lips. The collagen is injected into the edge of the lips, causing them to increase in size. Collagen can also be used to improve the appearance of hollow cheeks in patients suffering the side-effects of various drug treatments. The effects of collagen injections are only temporary, lasting about three to six months. The implanted collagen is gradually broken down and reabsorbed by the body.

There are a number of **synthetic** materials that can be used in the same way as collagen. However some people are allergic to the synthetic alternatives.

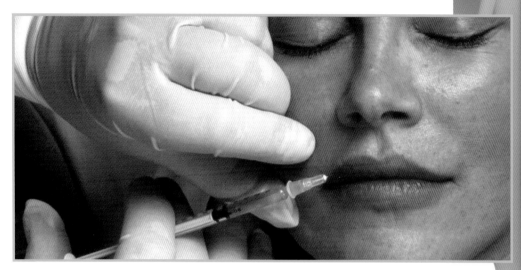

Collagen treatment involves simply injecting collagen into the skin using a very fine needle. The collagen fills out the skin and reduces the appearance of lines and wrinkles. Here the collagen is being injected to enhance the lips.

Fighting rejection

Although collagen can be injected into the body without ill effects, in other areas of plastic surgery **rejection** can be a major problem. Initially the grafted skin looks healthy and develops blood vessels, but soon the blood vessels break down and white blood cells gather around the skin graft (white blood cells help defend the body against disease). A few days later the skin graft begins to die off. It is killed by the white blood cells and other body defences, which do not recognize the graft as being part of the body.

Rejection of a graft can be prevented by using immunosuppressing drugs (drugs that stop the body's defences from attacking the graft). However, such drugs leave the patient vulnerable to infection because they affect the whole of the body's immune (defence) system, not just the part rejecting the graft.

Body reconstruction

A few decades ago, a person badly disfigured in a fire or an accident would have had to live with the change in their appearance and the problems associated with it. Today, advances in reconstructive surgery mean that a surgeon can often rebuild their body and improve their quality of life.

Injury, disease and defects

A surprising number of people may need treatment during their lifetime for injuries to their face or body. For example, each year in the UK more than a million people suffer facial injuries. The majority of serious facial injuries affect young people and are caused by accidents, fights or by drunken behaviour.

People may also require reconstructive surgery after treatment for **cancer**. Each year, thousands of women have to have cancer tissue removed from their breast, but surgeons can now use various techniques to reconstruct the breast afterwards (see pages 22–3). Mouth cancer can also cause disfigurement. It is the sixth most common cancer in the UK and it affects the tongue, cheeks and parts of the throat. Treatment for this cancer can involve the removal of large areas of diseased facial **tissues**. The patients have to deal with both the disease and a disfigured face.

Thousands of babies are born each year with **genetic** defects such as cleft lip and palate, double noses or displaced eyes. These are called congenital (inherited) deformities. In countries with a good standard of medical care, these defects are routinely treated by reconstructive surgery.

'It is thanks to micro-vascular surgery like this that we can now rebuild people's faces. Before, the bone grafts simply died. There has been a dramatic improvement in reconstruction over the past 10 or 15 years. We can now remove huge and aggressive cancers and instead of leaving patients with a gaping hole in the side of their faces, we can rebuild them.'

Iain Hutchinson, maxillofacial surgeon, Royal London Hospital

Replantation

Replantation is the term used to describe the reattachment of a severed hand, foot or even an entire limb. The operation to reattach the body part has to take place as quickly as possible after the accident that separated it. The severed part has to be kept clean and cold, although not freezing, as this delays the onset of irreversible tissue damage. The surgical team is often large and usually involves plastic surgeons and orthopaedic surgeons who deal with the bones and joints. First the surgical team identifies all the tendons, bones, nerves, arteries and veins and cleans them up ready for repair. Any crushed tissue has to be removed and broken bones have to be stabilized with metal plates. Using an operating microscope, the major arteries, veins and major nerves are repaired and rejoined with **sutures** that are barely half the diameter of a human hair.

After the operation the patient has to undergo an intensive programme of physiotherapy to restore muscle and nerve coordination. If the operation is successful the patient will regain normal sensation, good muscular control and strength. However, not all replantations are successful and the chance of success depends on the extent of the damage and the time since injury. A clean cut is likely to be more successful than an injury in which a limb is crushed.

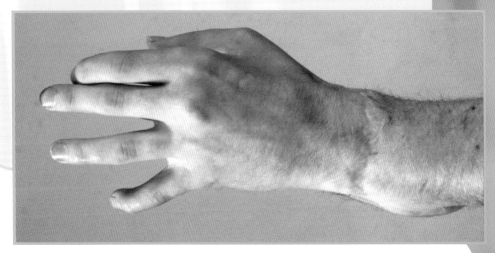

Surgeons trying to reattach a severed body part have to restore blood flow to the part within about ten hours of the time of injury, otherwise the tissues will die. The operation itself lasts many hours.

Cleft lip and palate

The word 'cleft' means 'split' or 'separation'. Congenital deformities such as cleft lip and cleft palate arise during the early stages of development of a **foetus**, when the two halves of the face develop separately and then join together. Sometimes the parts do not join properly and this results in a cleft. A cleft lip is a split in the upper lip between the mouth and nose. The baby is operated on within the first few months of life. The skin and muscles of its lip are simply rearranged. A cleft palate occurs when the roof of the mouth has not joined completely. A cleft palate can make it hard for a baby to suck, so it feeds slowly and takes in too much air. In this repair the tissues are joined together and no extra tissue is required from other parts of the body. These patients may require further surgery on their jaws and nose as they grow up.

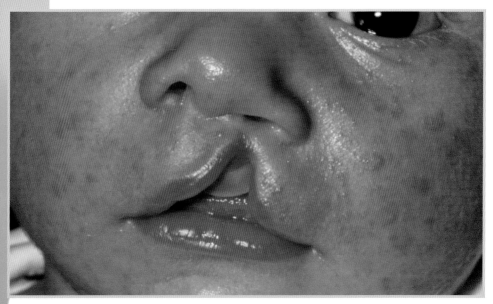

This baby has a cleft lip. The most common problem encountered during corrective surgery is when one side of the mouth and nose does not match the other side.

Longer limbs

Occasionally, children may be born with deformities such as a short femur (thigh bone) or legs of unequal length. This causes back pain and hip problems as the body tries to compensate. A new technique has been developed by Russian surgeons to replace missing bone and lengthen and straighten deformed bone. This technique can be used to

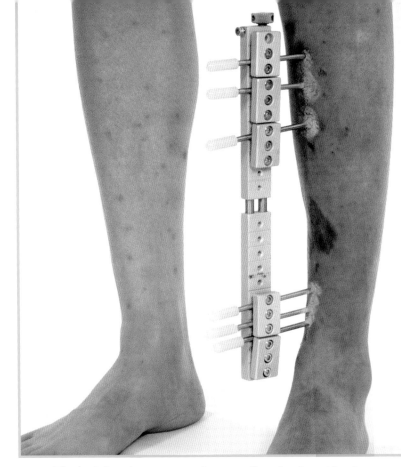

The limb lengthening procedure was first developed by the Russian surgeon Gavril Ilizarov in 1951. The picture shows the metal frame that holds the ends of the cut bone apart.

increase the height of very short people by as much as 30 cm in the leg and 12 cm in the arm. The procedure involves cutting the leg or arm bones and gradually pulling them apart. The cut bones are then held apart using metal splints so that the ends do not move. The body repairs the break by laying down new bone tissue to fill the gap. In doing this, the length of the limb bones is increased.

Many people lose their fingers in accidents at work. Sometimes they can be sewn back on, but often people have to live without their fingers. The bone lengthening technique has been adapted to stretch the stumps so that they regrow. The stump of the finger is broken and then pulled about a centimetre apart, leaving a gap in the bone. The finger is bolted in place with a metal frame, and the bone regrows to fill the gap. Unfortunately it is impossible to restore a completely severed finger to its original length, as the skin would not be able to stretch enough and joints would be needed to allow it to bend.

Rebuilding the face

The aims of facial reconstruction are to repair bone, facial muscles or skin, to restore functions such as swallowing or speech and to restore the appearance or symmetry of the face. In the early days of reconstructive surgery, metal was the material most generally used. Modern techniques now allow specialist facial surgeons to remove tissues from other parts of the body and use them to replace missing tissue on the face. The jaw and cheekbones, for instance, may be rebuilt using bones from the ribs and shoulders.

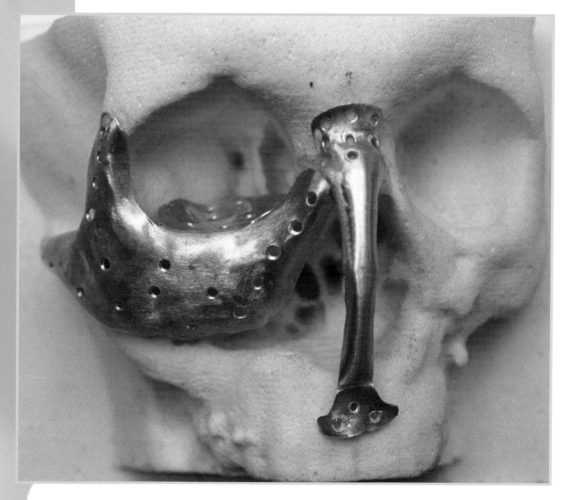

This picture shows the metal plates which were attached to the skull to form the cheek bone and nose during the rebuilding of a patient's face.

Reusing bone and tissue

In one particular case, a patient called Constance had a fast-growing mouth cancer that had spread through her jaw. The surgeon removed half her jaw and her cheek to ensure that all traces of the cancer were removed. The reconstruction was carried out at the same time. A section of bone from the top of her left shoulder blade was shaped into a jaw and fixed in place with a large metal plate and metal screws. Care was taken to ensure that the shoulder joint was left intact. A slice of skin from the back was removed to line the mouth. **Microsurgery** was used to join the tiny blood vessels attached to the **grafted** bone, each just two millimetres thick, to the carotid artery and jugular vein in the neck. Later Constance had false teeth implanted into her new jawbone and intensive speech therapy.

> 'My husband and I were obviously very scared when we discovered I had cancer, especially when we were told that to cure it the surgery would mean removing virtually half of my face. I was told very delicately but left with no illusion how serious it was. It is amazing how my face has been rebuilt so fantastically.'
>
> Constance, recovering from mouth cancer

Let's Face It

In 1977, Christine Piff was a busy mother with three young children. She developed a painful swelling in her left cheek, which was found to be a cancerous tumour. The cancer did not respond to radiotherapy or chemotherapy so she had to undergo surgery, which resulted in the loss of half her palate, her upper teeth and her left eye. During this traumatic period Christine felt that there was no one to talk to who had experienced something similar. She felt totally isolated.

In 1984 Christine launched a new charity, Let's Face It, to provide support for children and adults who have a different face. Today the charity is international with groups all over the world providing support. Their aim is to help people with facial disfigurements to share their experiences, to give them courage to cope with life and to educate the public to value the person behind every face.

Breast reconstruction

Approximately one in every nine women alive today in the UK will develop breast cancer. The treatment of this cancer involves the removal of the diseased tissue from the breast. Depending on the extent of the cancer, some women will need to have only part of a breast removed (a lumpectomy), but others may need to have the whole breast removed (a mastectomy).

Many women opt to have their breast reconstructed after such an operation. Studies have found that that the reconstruction helps women to recover from the cancer by making them feel normal.

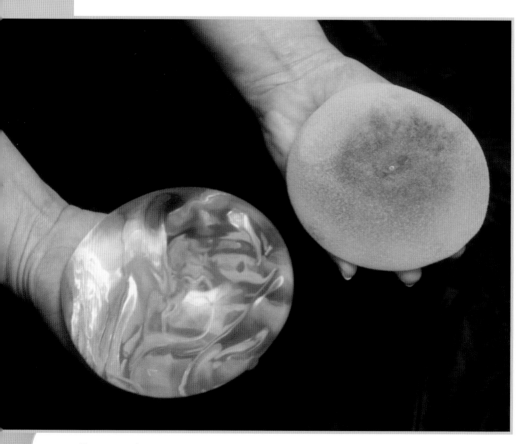

Breast implants come in various sizes and the surgeon must choose the most appropriate for the patient. The implant will be inserted under the skin.

Methods of re-building the breast

There are three methods of breast reconstruction:

Implants

Where enough breast tissue remains after surgery, it is possible to insert an implant under the skin. This is a plastic sac filled with either sterile salt solution or **silicone**.

Tissue expansion

Where there is little remaining breast tissue but the underlying muscles remain, a second method called tissue expansion can be used. This involves inserting an expandable implant under the chest muscle and gradually expanding it over a few months by injecting it with sterile salt water. This causes the skin and muscle to stretch. Once the desired expansion has been achieved, the expandable implant is replaced by a permanent silicone implant.

Flaps

The third method of reconstruction is used in cases where a woman has had all of the breast tissue and much of the underlying chest muscle removed. Areas of muscle and skin known as **flaps** are taken from the back or abdomen and used to rebuild the breast.

Breast reconstruction using flaps can be done in two ways. One way is to move the whole flap, with its blood supply still attached, by 'tunnelling' under the skin and on to the chest wall. The second method is called free flap reconstruction. In this method the flap is removed completely and the blood supply cut. This means that once the flap has been positioned on the chest wall, a new blood supply must be created, using blood vessels in the armpit or inside the chest. Very specialized microsurgery (see page 11) is needed to do this. The removal of flaps from the back or abdomen leaves large scars and the shape of the body may be altered by the loss of tissue. However, these areas are usually covered by clothing.

Coping with disfigurement

People cope with disfigurement in different ways. Some people
feel that their lives will never be normal until their disfigurement is
corrected. Others adapt to their disfigurement and come to believe
that it is an essential part of their character and that to alter it would
change them. They don't want a surgeon to put the disfigurement right.

There is no doubt that children suffer many emotional difficulties
from disfigurements, whether they are genetic or a result of injury.
A child may suffer from low esteem or may be subject to teasing and
bullying because he or she looks different. They may find it harder to
make friends and be reluctant to speak in class or the playground.
Often children are regularly absent from school to attend medical
appointments, and this disrupts their school life.

However many children are transformed after they have received
corrective surgery. One of the most common problems is ears that
stick out or 'bat ears'. Fortunately this is easily cured by simple
surgery, called otoplasty, in which the ears are pinned back.

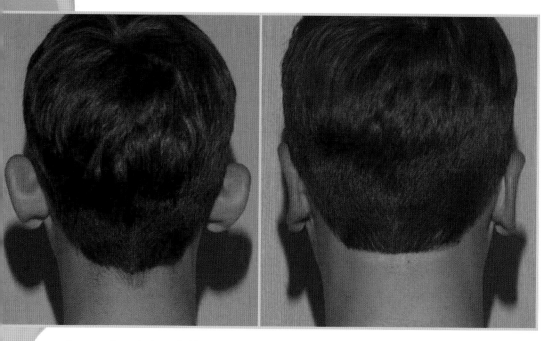

A young boy, before (left) and 18 months after surgery
to pin back his ears (right). In most cases, this procedure
– called otoplasty – is simple and highly effective.

Yes or no to reconstruction?

Rhonda's story

Rhonda is one of the many patients who feel happier with their reconstruction. Rhonda's abnormality started as a teenager when the right side of her jaw grew much longer than the left side. Her face was completely lopsided and her teeth did not meet. She was in continual pain and had difficulty eating. Her treatment started with the wearing of a brace to move the teeth into the right place. A year later she had the operation to rebuild her face. Her upper and lower jaws were broken and excess bone removed, her nose was broken and rebuilt in the right place. A bone graft and six metal plates were used to fill out her cheek bones and to screw her jaw back together. The surgeon avoided scarring by working from the inside, making cuts in her mouth and peeling the skin back to expose the facial bones. The most horrifying stage was probably Rhonda's appearance after the operation when her face was three times its usual size and she had drains and tubes running from it However, within six months her face had recovered.

> 'I am really pleased with the outcome and my friends all tell me I am much more confident now. It was certainly worth all the pain and discomfort, although I have to admit that I didn't think that immediately after the surgery.'
>
> Rhonda, 5 months after her surgery

Vicky's story

Vicky Lucas decided against reconstructive surgery. She suffers from a rare inherited disorder called cherubism, which affects the face. She found growing up with this disfigurement difficult, especially during **puberty** when her face became very large. So why has she turned down the opportunity to have a 'normal' face? She says she would rather be extraordinary than simply ordinary and wants people to appreciate that her face is integral to who she is. She has developed self-esteem and self-confidence and feels strongly that she shouldn't change her appearance just because of other people's attitudes towards her. Vicky has found that facial disfigurement is not just a medical issue, but a social issue as well. She realized that she was so unhappy, not because of the way her face looked, but because of the way some people would react to her face. She wants social attitudes to disfigurement to change.

> 'I am critical of a society that thinks the best thing to do – and the only thing to do – is for people with facial disfigurements to change themselves.'
>
> Vicky Lucas

A new skin

A healthy skin prevents the loss of fluid from the **tissues** beneath and is an effective barrier to infection. However, these functions are lost when the skin is burned.

Normal skin

The skin forms a protective covering over the body. It is made up of two layers, the **epidermis** and the **dermis**. The epidermis is the outermost part of the skin and is exposed to the environment.

Epidermal **cells** are made in the lowest layer of the epidermis. Here cells are continually growing and dividing. As new cells form, the older cells are pushed upwards. As they move up they die and become filled with a substance called keratin. Keratin is a tough, waterproof substance also found in nails, horns and hair. Hence, the outmost layer of skin is made up of dead cells that are hard and waterproof. The dead cells are continually worn off and are replaced by more cells from below. The tough top layer varies in thickness and is thickest on the soles of the feet.

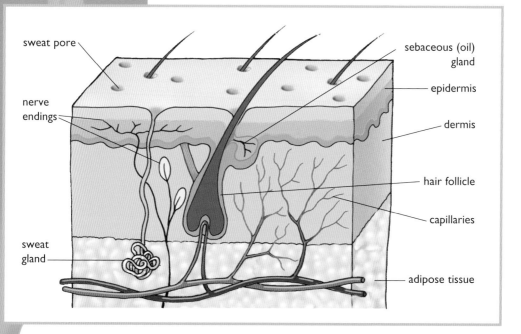

A cross-section through healthy skin. A typical square centimetre of skin contains 15 hairs, 15 sebaceous glands, 100 sweat glands, 55 centimetres of nerves and 500,000 dead and dying cells.

Some epidermal cells contain a dark brown pigment called melanin. Melanin protects the skin by absorbing harmful ultraviolet rays in sunlight. When the skin is exposed to ultraviolet light, the melanin spreads and the skin becomes darker and tanned. People who live in areas of the world where there is more sun have more melanin, which gives them a dark skin.

The dermis is much thicker than the epidermis. It is made up of mostly connective tissue. Connective tissue, as its name suggests, joins up all the structures found in the dermis, such as sweat glands, blood vessels and nerve endings. It is criss-crossed by strands of collagen and another **protein** called **elastin**. Together they give the skin elasticity and firmness.

Beneath the dermis is a layer of fat-filled cells called **adipose tissue**. This helps to keep the body warm by trapping heat. Adipose tissue also cushions the body from bumps and knocks.

Fat is also an energy reserve. If the body does not get enough energy from food, it breaks down the fat in adipose tissue to release energy.

Types of burns

The severity of a burn depends on how deeply it has affected the tissue. There are three categories of burn; superficial, partial thickness and full thickness (the most severe kind). These used to be called first-, second- and third-degree burns. In the case of superficial and partial thickness burns, the skin can regenerate (repair itself). However, full-thickness burns damage the dermis and so regeneration is not possible.

After severe burns, fluid is lost through the skin as the tissues swell and the blood vessels become leaky. Blood volume and blood pressure drop and this has a serious effect on the heart and circulation.

> 'Being burned is one of the most stressful things that can happen to the body. It incites an intense, inflammatory response, like when you hit your thumb with a hammer and it gets all red and swollen up…. The amount of energy it takes to keep going is equivalent to that of a marathon runner. Imagine running a marathon 24 hours a day and never being able to stop.'
>
> Dr David Heimbach, director of the Burns Unit at the Harborview Medical Centre, Seattle, USA

Skin grafts

Normally, people with full-thickness burns will need a skin **graft**. Skin grafts involve taking the full thickness of skin from healthy parts of the body and grafting that skin on to the burn wound. Sometimes a skin graft can be taken from the skin surrounding the injury, which gives a better match for colour and texture.

A graft is successful when new blood vessels and tissue form in the injured area. Unfortunately, skin grafts often fail. They may become infected and the tissues may die, or the whole skin graft may come away from the underlying skin as a result of pressure or movement.

Sometimes the damaged area lacks the blood supply needed for a successful skin graft. In these cases, a **flap** of skin together with underlying fat, blood vessels and sometimes muscle is moved from a healthy part of the body to the burn site. When the flap is attached the surgeons also reattach the blood vessels using **microsurgery**.

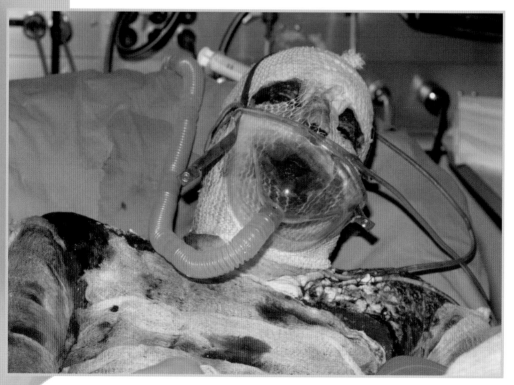

People with serious burns lose lots of liquid and often need intravenous fluids (fluids injected into their veins). They must be kept warm because the body cannot regulate its temperature properly. They must also be protected from germs, because the burned skin cannot protect itself from infection.

Some drawbacks

Skin grafts consisting of the epidermis and all the dermis (full-thickness grafts) can only be used for small areas. Also the grafts can only be taken from parts of the body were scarring will not be visible, as the removal of the flap leaves a noticeable scar.

Large areas of damaged skin are treated using split-thickness grafts (the epidermis and only part of the dermis). Split-thickness grafts have several disadvantages. They tend to contract or shrink during healing and they will not grow with the individual. The skin tends to be smoother and shinier than normal skin and it may be abnormally pigmented, either pale or white. If used to resurface large burns on the face, split-thickness grafts can produce an undesirable mask-like appearance. Finally, the wound created at the site from which the split-thickness graft is harvested is often more painful than the site to which the graft is applied.

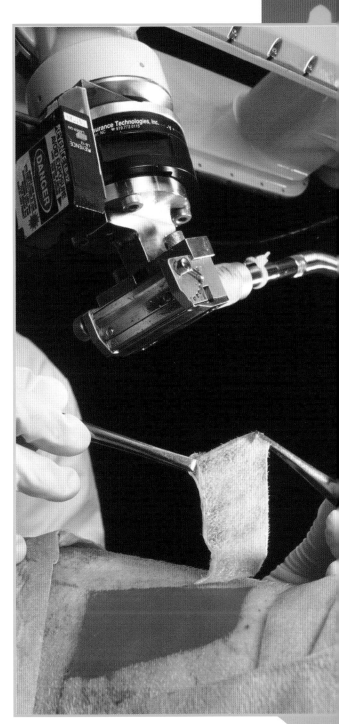

A skin-harvesting robot being tested on the skin of a pig. The robot is removing a thin layer of skin for use in skin grafts. Harvesting skin is a tricky procedure, and using a robot should make it easier to produce skin grafts in the future.

An artificial skin

If large areas of a person's skin are burned, there may not be enough healthy skin left to make grafts from. In the past, skin taken from dead people was used to make grafts in such cases. However there were problems, including **rejection** and infection. Nowadays, many burn patients are treated using artificial skin. One of the most useful artificial skins is one that can be used to treat full-thickness burns. This is a thin sheet containing collagen fibres and a substance that stimulates cell division and growth. The top layer of the artificial skin is **silicone**.

Growing a new layer

The burned skin is removed to reveal healthy tissue, then artificial skin is laid over the area, silicone layer on the outside. The artificial skin provides the framework for blood vessels and dermal skin cells to regrow into a new skin layer. Capillaries extend into the artificial skin providing it with a new blood supply, while skin cells move in from the surrounding healthy areas, gradually forming new skin. The silicone layer temporarily closes the wound and protects against infection, as well as controlling water and heat loss.

Within three weeks, a new layer of dermal skin is produced and the silicone layer can be removed. Then ultra thin pieces of epidermis are shaved off healthy areas of the person's skin and laid over the new dermal skin.

Unlike grafted skin, this new skin is flexible and will grow. The only limitation is that patients with large areas of new skin must avoid strenuous exercise in the sun, because the replacement dermis does not have sweat glands and hair follicles (roots). However, recent research has shown that hair follicles can be inserted into the new skin and they will start to grow hair.

> 'Burn patient survival rates have increased phenomenally over the last 10 years. If you had that type of success rate with AIDS, there would be Nobel prizes all over the place.'
>
> Scott Somers, head of the trauma and burn injury program for the US National Institutes of Health's Institute of General Medical Sciences

Culturing skin cells

Artificial skin cannot regenerate epidermis, only the dermis. Therefore it is still necessary to shave epidermal cells off the patient's own skin in order to complete the treatment. But now, epidermal cells can be grown in the laboratory and used to build an artificial epidermis.

First, a small area of skin is removed from a donor. The epidermal cells are separated and then grown in a special nutrient solution that stimulates them to multiply. Soon large numbers of epidermal cells, all identical to each other, have formed and they can then be stored in liquid nitrogen. The cells are combined with collagen, which provides a framework for the epidermis.

Cultured epidermis can be grown to more than 100 times the area of the original sample, and it takes only three weeks to grow a square metre. This may then be grafted on to parts of the body where the epithelial cells have been destroyed. The cultured epidermis is applied over the patient's wounds and covered with a traditional burn dressing. The wounds heal within one to two weeks after grafting.

With this method it should soon be possible to grow cultured epidermis from the patient's own skin cells. This would avoid any problems with rejection of the graft.

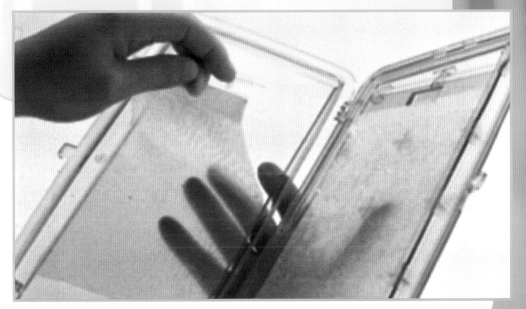

This artificial skin was made in a hospital laboratory in France. The thin layer of cultured epidermis is clipped to a piece of gauze to protect it until it is used.

Cosmetic facial surgery

Our face is on show all the time and it is probably the first thing people tend to notice. Whether we like it or not, society likes an attractive face. For instance, research has shown that attractive people are generally seen as being more intelligent and capable, so they often get better jobs. It is not surprising that people can become obsessed by the way they look, and that people who feel that their face is not attractive may want to change it.

The many adverts for cosmetic surgery in magazines make it sound easy. Some procedures can even be carried out in a lunch hour! Adverts may make people think that surgeons can work miracles, but not every face can be radically improved. There is also the risk that the surgery could go wrong.

An aging skin

People most often have facial treatment to remove signs of aging. As we get older, our skin becomes drier and loses its elasticity. The underlying **adipose tissue** becomes thinner, so the skin begins to sag. It looks and feels less supple and wrinkles appear.

A wide range of procedures to reverse signs of aging can be carried out. The face can be treated in various ways to remove the top layer of skin and reduce fine lines and wrinkles. However, the only way to get rid of baggy skin is to have some form of surgery. This could be anything from a relatively straightforward removal of bags under the eyes to a full **facelift**.

As people age, the skin gets baggy and wrinkles form around the eyes and mouth.

A fresh layer of skin

The least risky treatment for the face is a chemical peel. A chemical is applied to the skin, which causes the epidermal cells to blister and peel off over a period of 14 days. The peeled layers are replaced by new skin, which is smoother and brighter than before.

Each year more than one million people in the USA opt for micro-dermabrasion. A spray of very fine dust, such as fine aluminium oxide, is applied to the skin. The dust and the dead skin are then literally vacuumed off. This treatment removes the top layer of skin along with spots, minor lines, discolorations and large pores.

Photorejuvenation

Light treatments, known as photorejuvenation, are used to treat skin with sun damage. This damage could be broken capillaries, which look like tiny spider's webs on the surface of skin, or dark blotches and wrinkles. Photorejuvenation can also improve mild acne and reduce the size of large pores and fine lines.

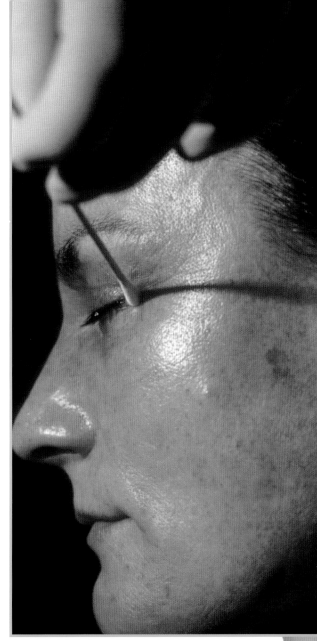

A chemical peel can sometimes cause the skin to lose its ability to tan, and people given these treatments have to stay out of the sun.

The treatment consists of a series of intense pulses of light of a specific **wavelength**. The light is focused on the target area of skin, for example a broken capillary. The heat from the pulse destroys the target, leaving the surrounding tissue untouched.

Botox®

Clostridium botulinum is a bacterium that produces one of the most deadly human toxins (poisons) known. Its main effect is to **paralyse** the muscles. However, this deadly toxin has some important uses, both in cosmetic surgery and in the treatment of diseases affecting muscles.

Botulinum toxin is used to treat medical conditions caused by excessive, involuntary contraction of muscles. It was originally approved to treat cross-eyes in adults and uncontrollable blinking. Some young people suffer from severe sweating of the palms and soles, and botulinum toxin has proved to be a very effective treatment because it paralyses the sweat glands. Some celebrities have been known to have injections in their armpits to prevent their designer clothes from being stained by sweaty patches!

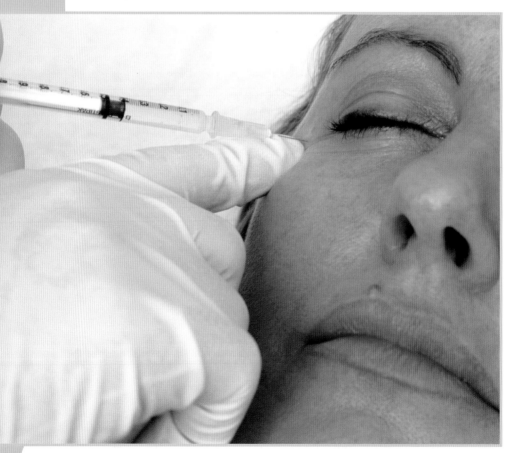

A fine needle is used to inject Botox® into the creases around the eyes. The muscles relax and the creases become less obvious.

Research is now looking at how botulinum toxin can be used to treat diseases of the nervous system, such as Parkinson's disease, Tourette's syndrome and multiple sclerosis, where patients can suffer from uncontrollable movements.

Weakening the muscles

However the most common use of botulinum toxin is in cosmetic procedures to get rid of wrinkles and frown lines on the face. The treatment is commonly called Botox®. A few drops of Botox® are injected into the muscle beneath a wrinkle. The toxin stops the muscle working, so the muscle weakens and the skin over it relaxes. The result is that wrinkles soften and may disappear, but it also means that people who have had Botox® treatment in their foreheads, for instance, cannot frown. The toxin wears off after several months, but with repeated treatments the effects last longer.

Problems can occur with Botox® injections. If they are given over a long period of time they can cause facial muscles to weaken and lead to one side of the face drooping.

Bags around the eyes

By far the most common plastic surgical procedure of the eyes is **blepharoplasty.** The procedure is relatively quick and has a high success rate. Blepharoplasty removes 'bags' above and below the eyes, under a local **anaesthetic**. For the upper lids, the surgeon makes an incision along the crease in the upper lid above the eyelashes, and removes excess skin and fat. On the lower lid, the surgeon can either make an incision right under the eyelashes, or inside the lid (this leaves no visible scar). Blepharoplasty is considered very safe, but serious complications such as dry eyes, drooping eyelids and even blindness can occasionally occur.

Rhinoplasty

Another popular facial procedure is **rhinoplasty** – 'a nose job'. The surgeon makes an incision to gain access to the bone and cartilage of the nose. This can be on the underside of the nose (the part separating the nostrils) or on the inside. The bone and cartilage are then sculpted to the desired shape by removing, adding or rearranging tissue. For example, a hump on the bridge of the nose is corrected by removing excess cartilage and trimming the bone.

Facelifts

As the face ages, the skin becomes less elastic, leading to wrinkles and sagging skin. Many older people have a facelift, or **rhytidectomy**, to try to reverse these signs of aging. With a successful facelift, the tightening of the skin and the underlying tissues can make a face look about 10 years younger, but if it goes wrong the face can look terrible.

Today's surgeons carry out facelifts using **endoscopes**. A number of small incisions are placed in areas where the most correction is needed. Usually this involves three or more 'puncture-type' incisions at the hairline. Incisions can also be hidden in the lower eyelids, in the upper gum line, beneath the chin and behind the ears. The endoscope allows the surgeon to release the muscles that produce frown lines and reposition the eyebrows at a higher level. **Liposuction** may be used to remove excess fatty tissue under the skin. Sometimes silicone implants may be positioned under the skin of the cheek or chin to improve the appearance of the face.

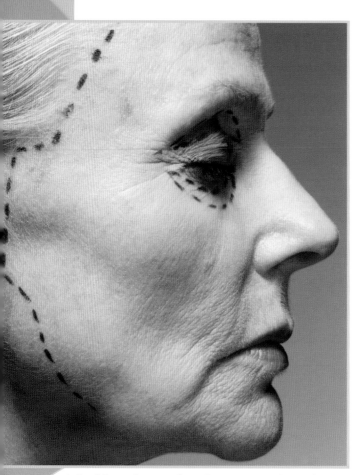

A facelift used to involve a long incision down the side of the forehead to the front of each ear and back into the hairline on the back of the head. This method often gave the patient a 'stretched' look, with the skin around the eyes being pulled to the sides.

'I'm not a facelift person. I just don't want to do it. For me the trade-off is that something of your soul in your face goes away. You end up looking body-snatched in the last analysis.'

Actor Robert Redford, 2002

'If it gives women more confidence, then I think that's great. Look at Cher: she's incredible. She might look a bit artificial, but at least she's not old and wrinkled. How many 60-year-olds do you see looking like that?'

Jo Asquith, businesswoman from London

A face gone wrong

Surgical mistakes in facial procedures are generally the most noticeable and often the most difficult to repair. Mistakes can leave the patient looking wooden or unnatural. The surgery may cause scarring and the distortion of facial features; for example, one eyebrow being higher than the other, the skin looking too tight or the whole face ending up asymmetric.

Often surgical errors can be repaired, but there has to be enough tissue for this to take place and the repair may be difficult. A poor nose job, for instance, can be impossible to put right. Patients may have to pay for the repair work, which might be more expensive than the original operation because the repair is technically more difficult. Even relatively simple procedures such as **collagen** implants in the lips can result in the lips looking unnaturally large. In some cases, patients experience an allergic reaction to the collagen and their lips and lower face swell up.

Some people undergo a series of surgical procedures in order to achieve major changes to their appearance - but the results can sometimes look unnatural.

The perfect body

In modern Western culture, slim is beautiful. Magazines, television and films all feature attractive young people with slim, toned bodies. For today's celebrities and aspiring celebrities, the 'perfect' body is vitally important. Many feel that they will only succeed if they have the 'right' body for the camera. They exercise and diet, and if that doesn't work, they resort to cosmetic surgery.

We have already seen that ideas of beauty differ between cultures, but the Western concept of beauty is spread around the world through television and film. The native women of Fiji used to prefer rounded bodies, but in 1995 American television arrived in the islands and within a short time many Fijian girls were describing themselves as too big or too fat.

Celebrity looks

For today's generation, the ideal body is probably one they have seen on television or in a celebrity magazine. It is not uncommon for young women to turn up at a consultation with a cosmetic surgeon complete with pictures torn from magazines. They ask the surgeon for breasts or lips like supermodels or the curvy body of *Tomb Raider* star, Angelina Jolie. These ideal women often have features that, though they may be natural, look as though they have been surgically or computer-enhanced.

Sometimes the features of celebrities look great with makeup and reproduced in a photo or on television, but they can look distorted in real life. With the advances in surgical techniques it is becoming possible to create a body with the desired shape. For example, using the latest methods of **liposuction**, a surgeon can virtually sculpt a person's body to look like someone else. However there is the risk that the new 'shape' could look odd on another person.

So why do people want to change their bodies? They may feel that a slimmer body would give them a better self-image, which would help them to become confident and happier. They may feel that they would be more able to participate in sport and other activities.

Designer exercise

The traditional ways of improving one's body shape or appearance is through diet and exercise. Dieting is one way to lose weight, while exercise helps with slimming and also tones the muscles. During exercise the body burns fuel and this leads to fat reserves being used, hence a slimmer body. Weight training can build up muscle strength and mass, and this creates a greater change in body shape. Bodybuilders combine exercise with diet to increase their muscle bulk and remove fat deposits.

Increasing numbers of people in rich, developed countries are joining gyms to keep themselves fit. Hours of carefully designed exercise can lead to a muscular, sculpted body. However, many people have neither the time nor the single-mindedness to reach high levels of fitness. Instead they may turn to surgery to improve the way their body looks.

Instant results

Exercise takes time and a lot of effort and willpower. Many people want an instant change rather than a gradual one, and they turn to cosmetic surgery for help. In other cases it does not matter how much a person exercises, they may never be able to change the appearance of certain body features. Some men, for instance, suffer from gynecomastia, an inherited condition in which they have enlarged, fatty breasts. Men with gynecomastia may also turn to surgery. Oversized breasts can also be a problem for women. The weight of the breasts can cause back, neck or shoulder pain and some large-breasted women are unable to participate in sports. The only way they can overcome this is to resort to surgery.

At the Seoul Olympics in 1988, Canadian sprinter Ben Johnson won the men's 100 metres final in 9.79 seconds. The time was a record that remained unbeaten until 2002. However, drugs tests showed that Johnson had used steroids to achieve his record-breaking time. His gold medal was given to second-place Carl Lewis, and Johnson was banned from international athletics.

Bodybuilding and drug abuse

Drugs known as anabolic steroids (anabolic means building up) can speed up bodybuilding and enhance body shape. The **hormone testosterone** is a natural anabolic steroid, produced in a man's **testes**. One of its many roles is to increase muscle bulk. The first **synthetic** anabolic steroids were developed in the 1940s. They were first used to help the recovery of the many severely malnourished people released from prisoner-of-war and concentration camps at the end of World War II. In recent years a number of bodybuilders, athletes and other sports people have abused these drugs, using them to artificially improve their performance.

Anabolic steroids

Anabolic steroids work by increasing the amount of **protein** that the body produces, some of which goes into making more muscle. They also stimulate the production of red blood cells and this increases the quantity of oxygen carried in the blood. Like most drugs, anabolic steroids have numerous side-effects. For example they can cause acne, increased infertility in males and increased masculinity and menstrual disturbances in females.

Insulin

Recently, a number of bodybuilders have started to use **insulin** as well as steroids. Insulin is one of two hormones that control the level of the sugar glucose in the blood. It is used medically to treat **diabetes**. Insulin causes glucose to be taken up from the blood into liver cells, where it is converted to a **carbohydrate** called glycogen. Glycogen is a quick-release energy store – it can be broken down during exercise to provide energy. In order to build up extra glycogen stores, some athletes and bodybuilders take glucose and insulin simultaneously for a couple of hours shortly before a competition. However, the insulin can cause blood glucose to fall to dangerously low levels, causing the individual to collapse and go into coma. Death can result.

Unfortunately insulin is readily available and its use is not illegal, although it has been banned by bodybuilding associations and by the International Olympic Committee.

'I just wish people could be honest about taking steroids. Then they could compete with other people who are taking them... You have virtually no chance against them if you're a natural bodybuilder.'
Sonia Schulenburg, leading British bodybuilder 2002

Abdominal plastic surgery

Abdominal plastic surgery includes procedures to remove and tighten excess skin, fat and muscle **tissue**. Some people choose to have abdominal plastic surgery in order to get rid of folds of loose skin that form after weight loss. Others have surgery because they have tried dieting and exercise, but have stubborn areas of fat remaining.

Abdominal plastic surgery usually involves liposuction, or a 'tummy tuck' (abdominoplasty), or both. A tummy tuck reduces the size of the stomach area. However, the incisions can be large and the procedure can take time to heal. In some cases, abdominal plastic surgery is performed on a small area of the stomach, a procedure called a 'mini-tuck'. This removes fat and tightens skin and muscles below the tummy button.

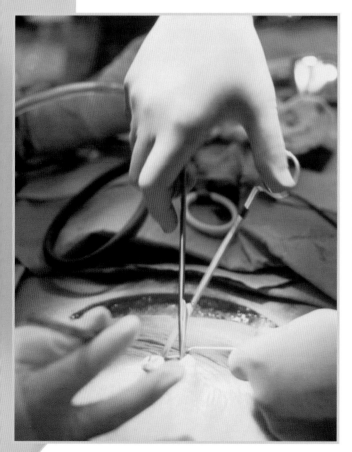

Some people opt for a complete lower-body lift, which is a major procedure that leaves a large scar. The surgeon makes an incision around the entire circumference of the abdominal area, so that excess skin can be removed and the hip, thigh and buttock areas can be lifted. The result of the procedure is tightening of the back, hip and abdominal tissues.

Surgeons performing an abdominal 'mini-tuck'. This kind of operation is less serious than a full tummy tuck because it involves only small incisions. A mini-tuck is usually combined with liposuction.

Breast surgery

In recent years, breast enlargement has become one of the most frequently performed cosmetic procedures for women. Once again, the fact that a number of successful female celebrities have had breast enlargements has resulted in more women opting for the operation. In 2000 alone, more than 250,000 woman in the USA had the operation. The current method involves the use of implants filled with either saltwater or **silicone**. The surgeon makes an incision and slips a sterilized implant into a pocket under the breast.

A woman undergoing breast enlargement has to be aware of the risks. The incisions will leave scars, and there are sometimes side-effects, such as swelling, bruising, bleeding, infection and numbness or changes in feeling. She should also know that she may not be able to breast-feed after surgery, due to damage to the blood supply to the nipple.

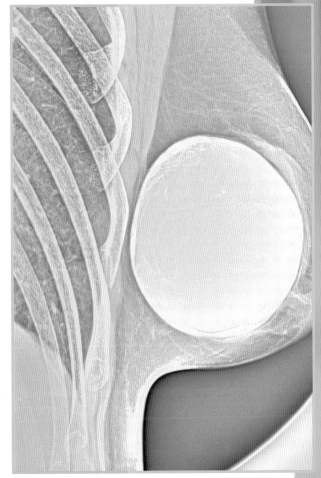

Men with gynecomastia (fatty breasts) may have an operation to reduce their breasts. In some cases the fat can be removed simply by liposuction, but usually there is some glandular tissue rather than just **adipose tissue**. In these cases an operation is needed to remove the glandular tissue.

'Cosmetic surgery remains a bit of a lottery. Our investigation showed that [patient information about the risks involved] was severely lacking in many cases.'
Sue Freeman, *Health Which?* magazine, following an investigation into eleven cosmetic clinics in London

This X-ray through a woman's breast after enlargement surgery shows the implant in the breast.

Problem implants

Silicones are **polymers** made from the element silicon. Silicone comes in a variety of forms, including gels (jelly-like materials) that are ideal for implants. During the 1980s, thousands of women had silicone breast implants. Then in 1992, as a result of health scares, silicone breast implants were withdrawn in the USA. Silicone implants were replaced with implants containing salt water.

There seemed to be a number of problems with silicone implants. The most serious were highlighted in a study that showed a link between silicone implants, breast **cancer** and **autoimmune diseases**. Since that time more research has been carried out and silicone has been declared to be safe. Silicone implants have not yet been reintroduced to the USA, but they are used widely in Europe.

There are two other problems with implants. First, silicone implants do not last forever. Studies have found that as many as one in six implants burst after about five years and had to be removed. The second problem is capsular contracture. This is the formation of excessive scar tissue around the implant, which leads to hardening and a change in shape of the breast. Further surgery has to be carried out to remove scar tissue and replace the implant.

The J-Lo factor

Recently, the curvaceous backside of pop star and actress Jennifer Lopez caused a stir in the world of cosmetic surgery. Young women were demanding 'a butt like J-Lo' and there was an upsurge in the number of woman wanting buttock implants. The procedure involves the insertion of solid silicone implants between the main buttock muscles and their covering tissue. This creates a fuller and more rounded buttock. However there are problems with these implants. Unlike a breast implant, the buttocks are subjected to more pressure so there is greater likelihood of the implant bursting. There may also be damage to the sciatic nerve running down the leg, which could lead to serious disability. Most patients have to wear a 'compression girdle' for several weeks while the tissues of the buttocks heal. Also, they cannot sit up properly for several weeks until the post-operative swelling goes down.

> '... the implants don't do well on an area we put so much pressure on like the buttocks.'
> Dr Ed Luce, President of the American Society of Plastic Surgeons and Chief of Plastic Surgery at University Hospitals of Cleveland, Ohio, USA

Although there has been a great deal written in the press about Jennifer Lopez's curvaceous backside, there has not been a general change in the Western idea that extremely thin is beautiful.

Cosmetic concerns

Cosmetic surgery is a very competitive business, but for the patient, it is full of pitfalls. Many people are won over by the glossy adverts in magazines and newspapers, or the websites devoted to cosmetic surgery with their promises of improved looks. Often people commit themselves to surgery without investigating further.

Cut-price surgery

People may spend their life's savings on cosmetic surgery. A relatively simple Botox® injection can cost £200 and this has to be repeated every few months. A nose job can cost between £2000 and £4000, a breast enlargement costs up to £5000, while a **facelift** can cost anything up to £7000.

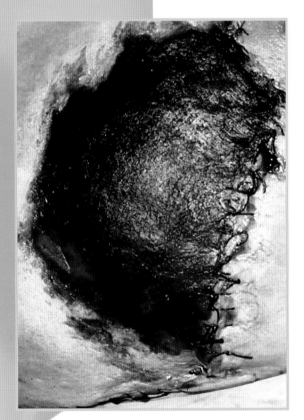

As costs rise, many people are tempted to go overseas where clinics offer the same procedures for as little as a quarter of the usual price. Some people opt to combine a holiday with surgery, the so-called 'sun, sea, sand and **scalpel** specials'. Some people decide to go ahead with the procedures without checking the qualifications of the surgeon or the facilities offered by the clinic. Some of the procedures carried out are risky and the clinic may not have the proper backup facilities if something goes wrong. In such clinics post-operative care is often limited and the patient may be sent home within a few hours.

One of the biggest risks in cosmetic surgery is infection. Some clinics have poor hygiene standards and surgical equipment may carry infectious germs. Poor-quality clinics can be less than helpful when things go wrong. Patients are often forced to go to their own doctor for treatment.

New regulations

Sub-standard cosmetic surgery is taking place in clinics around the world. In the UK over the last 13 years, more than £7 million has been paid out in compensation to people who have made claims over poor cosmetic surgery. In an attempt to improve standards, new regulations have been introduced in the UK by the National Care Standards Commission.

Even celebrities can suffer the consequences of poor surgery. One victim of a cosmetic procedure is actress Lesley Ash who had a **collagen** injection in her lips that went wrong. Now she has undergone further treatments to rectify the damage.

Liposuction – the risks

Risk is an important factor when considering cosmetic surgery. Most patients are perfectly healthy before surgery, therefore surgeons have to take all the possible risks into consideration when recommending surgery to a patient. For many years, **liposuction** was one of the more popular but risky cosmetic procedures. During the mid 1990s in the USA one in every 139 patients experienced a complication such as a blood clot, fluid loss, infection or an adverse reaction to the **anaesthetic.** There were even some deaths. The problem was linked to the sudden rise in the popularity of liposuction, which meant that many surgeons were carrying out the procedure with insufficient training and experience. However, the situation is improved and the number of complications and deaths has declined. A recent study in the USA has found that less than one in 47,000 people undergoing liposuction died, and the complication rate has fallen to one in 384.

Unrealistic expectations

People decide that they want cosmetic surgery because they want to change part of their body for the better. They have an expectation that the operation will improve their appearance. People may undergo surgery thinking that they are going to look much younger or end up several sizes smaller. If the surgeon does not give a realistic idea of what can be achieved, the patient is bound to be disappointed by the surgery.

Cosmetic surgeons have to make difficult decisions when advising patients on surgical procedures. Surgeons are often visited by young women who are unhappy about the way they look and request

When deciding on whether to have plastic surgery, the advice given by doctors cannot always be relied on. Most cosmetic surgery is carried out privately, with the patient paying the doctor. Doctors stand to gain financially from the operation so they may be tempted to encourage patients to have a procedure even though it may not be in the patients' best interest.

operation after operation to improve an already attractive body. If they are turned away, they visit more surgeons, or they may have surgery in a country where the regulations are less strict.

In many cases, there is nothing wrong with the person's appearance and cosmetic surgery is not always the answer. Some patients have a psychological problem that really needs psychiatric treatment, not surgery.

In a few cases, people can have problems coming to terms with their much-improved appearance after plastic surgery, especially if they had got used to living with a badly disfigured face.

Too young for surgery?

In 2001, a programme on British television raised a storm of controversy when it reported that a teenager wanted to have her breasts enlarged when she turned 16, even though her breasts would not be fully developed by that age. The girl believed that she needed bigger breasts if she was to succeed later in life and that they would boost her self-confidence. Her parents supported her and agreed to pay for the surgery.

So was this girl unusual in wanting to improve her looks? Surgeons report seeing more teenagers who want to alter their appearance. Most agree that procedures such as nose reshaping or pinning the ears back are appropriate for young people with awkward features. But what about breast enlargement, eyelid surgery or the removal of fat from the stomach and thighs?

Advertising and entertainment media can have a tremendous influence on young people. They need careful guidance from parents and doctors when making decisions about plastic surgery. Sometimes parents can themselves be part of the problem. They want what is best for their child and often believe that cosmetic surgery is one way of improving the child's chances in life. One doctor reports that on asking the question 'Why don't you like your ears?', a child answered 'My father thinks they're too big'. Surgeons have to deal carefully with cases such as this. They may insist on a waiting period to allow the young person to change their mind.

'It's important to take time and weigh up the risks and benefits.'
British Association of Plastic Surgeons (BAPS)

Future body

In the film *Face/Off*, Nicholas Cage and John Travolta have their faces swapped using **laser** technology. This may seem far-fetched, but it could be possible in the not too distant future. And face **transplants** are only the start. The body will always age, regardless of how much plastic surgery is carried out, so people may turn to more extreme ways of slowing down the aging process — perhaps even stepping into a new body! Such a development is perhaps far in the future, but other advances are being tested today.

Growing fat

Why use a **synthetic** implant when fat can be taken from other parts of the body and used to enlarge the breast or fill the cheeks? At the moment fat is not used for implants because it breaks down within the body. But in the near future we may be able to remove **adipose tissue** from one part of the body, grow it to the right shape in the laboratory, then insert it into the breasts or buttocks.

Cultured adipose tissue could be used in facial reconstruction and face-lift surgery too, to fill sunken cheeks, lines and wrinkles. The **collagen** implants used today break down and have to be replaced, but adipose fillers would not have this problem.

In the film *Face/Off*, actors Nicholas Cage and John Travolta swap faces. The film is science fiction, but most of the technology to do such an operation is already available.

Silkworms

Until adipose implants are available, surgeons will continue to use collagen – and a new source has been developed in Japan. Silkworms have been **genetically modified** so that instead of spinning cocoons made of pure silk, they produce cocoons that are ten per cent collagen. The collagen is easy to extract, so this method could be used in the future to produce large amounts of collagen cheaply.

Stem cells

Further in the future, advances in technology could allow plastic surgeons to produce cosmetic implants that would make adipose tissue implants seem primitive. **Cells** could be taken from the patient, grown in the laboratory and then formed into implants for insertion back into the body.

The cells that are of greatest interest to scientists are **stem cells**. In humans, the cells of specialized tissues such as muscles and nerves become unable to divide once they are fully developed. But the cells are constantly dying and need to be replaced. New cells are supplied by stem cells, which continually divide to provide the replacements for cells that die.

Some stem cells have the ability to form other specialized cell types as they multiply. This means that a group of stem cells could be used to produce a number of different **tissues.** Some might be used to grow new bone, while others might form muscle. The stem cells would be grown on a framework to create an implant that would fit perfectly. The body would not reject the implant or form scar tissue around it because it would be made by the body's own cells.

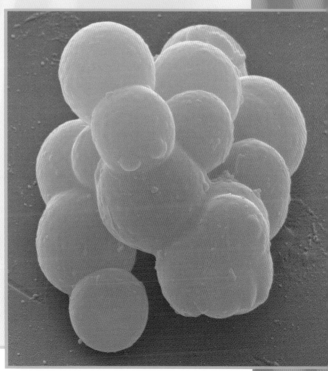

Face transplants and beyond

According to some leading surgeons, full face transplants are no longer science fiction fantasy. They believe that such an operation would be technically feasible. New drugs make it possible to stop the body's immune system rejecting a transplanted face. **Microsurgery** could transplant new skin, bone, nose, chin, lips and ears from dead donors to patients disfigured by accidents, burns or **cancer**. One of the possible techniques would involve transplanting a 'skin envelope' of fat, skin and blood vessels on to the existing bone, leaving the patient with many of their own features. A more complex procedure would be required to transplant the underlying bone as well, so that the patient would end up resembling the donor.

But would there be any donors? Many people when asked said that they could accept the procedure but few would be willing to donate their face after dying. A large part of a person's identity is connected to their face, so face transplants could also cause psychological problems for the patient receiving the face.

> 'There are so many people without faces ... but we are all so much more than just a face ... you don't take on their personality. You are still you. If we can donate other organs of the body then why not the face? I can't see anything wrong with it.'
>
> Christine Piff, who founded the charity Let's Face It
> after suffering a rare facial cancer

A whole new body?

Face transplants are just the start. Some doctors are thinking of more radical surgery which would involve transplanting the whole head, including the brain. Such a procedure could be used to treat people whose bodies rather than their brains are diseased. Obviously this would be an incredibly complex process and beyond current abilities. But with the advancement of microsurgery, it seems that nothing will be impossible in the future. The Open University's Millennium Project has worked with experts to forecast the changes we will see in the new millennium. It predicts that in the future organ manufacturing skills could be used to build a new body to 're-house' the brain.

In fact, the first brain transplant has been carried out – on a monkey. In 2001, Professor Robert White, from Cleveland, Ohio, USA, transplanted the head containing the intact brain of a monkey on to another monkey's body and the animal survived for some time after the operation. Professor White would like to be able to carry out a similar operation on humans but many in the medical field consider the experiments to be grotesque.

Virtual reality

Computers already have an important role to play in plastic surgery, in particular the area of **virtual reality**. Virtual reality aims to show the user a computer-generated environment. The user wears a helmet linked to a computer with a head-mounted display showing the scene. They may wear gloves, or even a body suit, that is also connected up so that they can 'feel' the environment as well as hearing and seeing it.

Soon there will be virtual reality trainers for plastic surgeons. For example, trainee surgeons will be able to practice medical procedures such as making incisions and joining up blood vessels using virtual reality, before operating on a live patient.

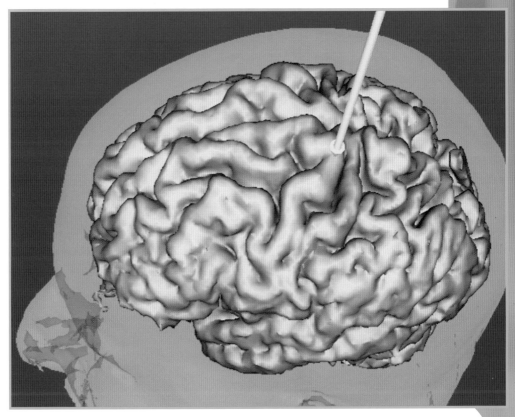

In virtual reality, three-dimensional images allow the surgeon to visualize an operation before carrying it out. By wearing virtual reality gloves, the surgeon can even get the feel of carrying out the actual procedure.

Simulations

Patients will increasingly use virtual reality to see exactly how their new cheeks, breasts or lips will look. Once they have created their very own 3-D character on screen, the medical team will use it to make accurate implants. The surgery itself could be carried out by robots, via remote control, allowing specialists to operate on patients hundreds of kilometres away – or even in another country. Robots are already being used in some kinds of surgery, so it will not be long before they are being used in plastic surgery.

Virtual reality suits

A virtual reality suit has devices that transmit the sight, sounds and sensations of the artificial world to the user and send information about what he or she is doing to the computer. Inside the helmet are tiny TV screens that allow users to 'see' 360° as they turn their heads. The sensory glove sends information about a user's hand movements to the computer, which then instructs the glove to create a sensation, such as tapping a finger on a hard surface.

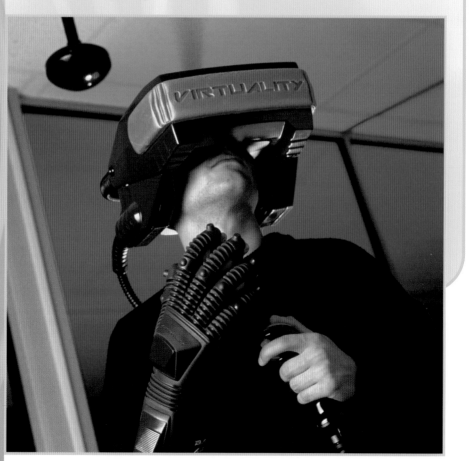

Virtual-reality simulations have already been used to reconstruct the face of a young boy whose features were destroyed by cancer. First the patient was placed in a **magnetic resonance imaging (MRI) scanner** to obtain detailed images of the tissues inside his head. Then the imaging data was fed into the simulation, which allowed the surgeons to visualize how the soft tissues fitted over the bone and how the face would appear after surgery. By practising the procedures beforehand using a simulation, the surgeons were much better able to carry out the actual surgery. In future, with more computer power, surgeons will be able to work on larger areas of the body.

Perfect children

As our ability to manipulate genes improves, it is possible that within a few generations, parents may be able to 'design' their own children. This would be the ultimate form of body sculpture – designing a new individual from scratch. However, this raises many issues. Should parents be able to eliminate defective genes from their embryos? Should they be allowed to go further and create a the child with a particular appearance? Or should society prevent any form of **genetic** manipulation and leave it to nature? Is the manipulation of an embryo any different to **selective breeding**?

Perhaps the most worrying aspect of **genetically engineering** children is that it would probably reduce the genetic diversity of the human race – how different we are genetically from one another. It is likely that, given the choice, people would choose a limited range of characteristics for their children. In time, some genetic characteristics would be lost altogether. Also, a population of people who were genetically similar would be less able to deal with unexpected changes in their environment, such as the outbreak of a new disease.

'As soon as the geneticists can tweak an embryo to produce a blonde, blue-eyed, long-limbed baby, there will be a customer. But the future population of Barbie dolls won't be necessarily content. In my experience perfection often leads to more insecurity – and ultimately more surgery.'

Kathy Phillips, Health and Beauty Director at Vogue

'Design a body? It may be possible. I can do anything.'

Kevin Montgomery, Computer Engineer, National Biocomputation Center, Stanford University, California, USA

Concluding thoughts

Sue Morgan Elphick suffered from a facial deformity that made her lower jaw protrude beneath her upper. At the age of 30, she was a nurse at St Bartholemews Hospital, London, working for a plastic surgeon who specialized in reconstructing faces. One day the surgeon suggested he should reconstruct *her* face. To do this, he had to break nearly every bone in her face, and then fasten them together again with strips of titanium.

The reconstruction was incredibly painful, but a great success. Before her surgery, Sue was often thought of as miserable, although in fact she was funny and bubbled with life. Today Sue is an energetic, attractive woman. This illustrates the degree to which we form our opinions of a person's character on the basis of their looks.

> *'I felt as though I was a walking freak-show. I was made to feel like a freak, and I really took it to heart. When I was a teenager no-one wanted to know me. I never got any attention. I never had any boyfriends.'*
> Sue Morgan Elphick

A cosmetic future?

Advances in reconstructive surgery have filtered through into cosmetic surgery, leading to huge increases in the demand for cosmetic surgery over the last ten years. Cosmetic plastic surgery is a lucrative business and clinics are springing up around the world. By far the greatest number of these are in the USA and Europe, but more clinics are being set up in Eastern European countries, Australia, South Africa, Mexico, South America and Asia.

A worrying trend is that the age of the patients opting for cosmetic surgery is decreasing. In the past, the majority of patients were older women wanting to look younger. Now increasing numbers of younger people, both men and women, are opting for plastic surgery in order to improve their appearance. It is becoming almost fashionable to have cosmetic surgery.

We have seen how reconstructive surgery has made enormous advances, allowing surgeons to reconstruct bodies and faces, and in the process often rebuild their lives. Further advances in technology will undoubtedly mean that plastic surgeons will be able to carry out even more adventurous surgery in the future.

The huge market for cosmetic surgery is a result of our society's obsession with image. We are surrounded every day by pictures of flawless faces and bodies. In the future our obsession with perfect looks could be taken further, as **genetic engineering** allows us to create 'designer babies'.

Accepting difference

In our society, people with disfigurements are seen as abnormal and suffer from other people's attitudes towards them. For many people with a disfigured face or body, it is the way other people react to them that bothers them most, not their actual disfigurement. Plastic surgery often helps people with disfigurements, but perhaps a better approach would be to educate people to accept physical differences, and look beyond the surface appearance to the personality beneath. If we valued people less for their appearance, perhaps fewer people would feel the need for cosmetic surgery in the first place.

Timeline

1827   American Dr John Peter Mettauer performs the first cleft palate operation in North America with instruments he designed himself.

1838   The term 'plastic surgery' is first used in the surgical manual *Handbuch der Plastischen Chirurgie*, published by Zeiss.

1881   American Edward Talbott Ely performs the first correction of protruding ears on a 12-year-old boy at the Manhattan Eye, Ear and Throat Hospital in New York, USA.

1896   Jacques Joseph (born Jakob Lewin Joseph) reduces and pins back the ears of a boy with large protruding ears. Two years later he carries out a nose reduction on another patient. He becomes known as the father of modern facial plastic surgery and a leading facial surgeon in Europe.

1914–18   During World War I, French army surgeon, Hippolyte Morestin, establishes a treatment centre for wounded soldiers in France. A similar unit is set up at Aldershot Military Army Hospital in Hampshire by Sir Harold Gillies and Sir William Arbuthnot Lane. This becomes the first centre of facial plastic surgery.

1940   The botulinum toxin is isolated.

1949   First breast implant using a polyvinyl alcohol sponge is carried out.

1961   The use of **silicone** implants is reported by Thomas Cronin.

1962   Ronald A Malt performs the first successful replantation of an entire limb, on a 12-year-old boy whose arm had been severed in a train accident.

1964   Dr Harry Buncke reports the first successful rabbit-ear replantation to the Plastic Surgery Research Council Meeting in Kansas City, Kansas, USA. This was the first successful reattachment of an amputated part involving blood vessels less than one millimetre in diameter.

1969   Dr Harry Buncke and Donald McLean perform the first successful microvascular tissue **transplant** during the repair of a defect of the scalp.

1970	Professor Earl Owen carries out the first rejoining of an amputated finger.
1972	Two Japanese surgeons, Harii and Ohmori carry out the first successful free skin **flap** transplant in a human.
1974	Dr Giorgio Fischer carries out **liposuction**.
1976	Injectable **collagen** is used for the first time.
1986	Dr David Heimbach at Harborview Medical Centre, Seattle, USA leads the team carrying out the world's first clinical trial of a new artificial skin, later called Integra.
1987	Jeffrey Klein introduces a new method of liposuction that involves the injection of an **anaesthetic** liquid. This allows for more fat to be removed, while at the same time reducing blood loss.
1989	Botulinum toxin is approved by the Food and Drug Administration (FDA) in the USA for the treatment of cross-eyes in adults, uncontrollable blinking and certain facial spasms.
1992	The FDA in the USA declares a temporary ban on silicone implants.
	Monte Keen, the director of facial, plastic and reconstructive surgery at the Columbia Presbyterian Medical Center, New York, USA is the first doctor to use botulinum toxin as an anti-wrinkle treatment.
1998	Dow Corning, one of the largest manufacturers of silicone breast implants, settles a class action lawsuit for $3.2 billion for 170,000 women who suffered serious side effects after surgery.
1999	The Institute of Medicine in the USA issues a 400-page report which concludes that silicone breast implants do not cause major illnesses. The main concerns include the tendency for the implant to leak or rupture, which leads to infections, hardening and breast tissue scarring.
2001	Professor Robert White, from Cleveland, Ohio, USA transplants the head containing the brain of a monkey into another monkey's body and the animal survives for a few days.
2002	Silkworms are given the gene to produce collagen. The modified silkworms produce cocoons that are ten per cent collagen.

Glossary

adipose tissue tissue made up of cells containing fat

anaesthesia using drugs (anaesthetics) to cause the loss of sensation and consciousness before surgery

autoimmune diseases diseases in which the body produces antibodies that act against its own cells; for example, rheumatoid arthritis

blepharoplasty (pronounced 'blef-ar-o-plas-te') cosmetic procedure carried out on the eyes to remove baggy skin

cancer disease where the abnormal and uncontrollable growth of cells forms a malignant tumour or growth

carbohydrates molecules that contain carbon, hydrogen and oxygen, such as glucose, starch and glycogen. Carbohydrates are used by the body as a source of energy.

cell functional unit of the body, consisting of a nucleus and cytoplasm bound by a membrane

collagen type of protein which has a structural role in the skin

cultured cells or microorganisms that are grown in the laboratory

dermis lower layer of the skin which contains structures such as sweat glands and capillaries

diabetes medical condition in which the pancreas fails to produce insulin, causing the blood glucose levels to rise

elastin type of protein that has elastic properties. It can be stretched and, when released, return to its original length.

endoscope surgical instrument for viewing the internal parts of the body

epidermis outermost layer of the skin with cells that contain the pigment melanin

facelift cosmetic surgery in which the skin is tightened to remove wrinkles from around the eyes, nose and mouth

flap section of skin with muscle, blood vessels and nerve attached which is taken from a healthy part of the body and used to rebuild a damaged part

foetus unborn baby of a mammal. In the case of a human baby, the embryo becomes a foetus at eight weeks.

genetic inherited

genetic engineering process by which the DNA (genetic makeup) of an organism is altered by scientists. This can be achieved by inserting a gene taken from another organism or by removing a gene.

genetically modified DNA that has been altered artificially in the laboratory

graft to transplant living tissue on to a damaged area of the body; for example, a skin graft in which healthy skin tissue, taken either from the same person or a donor, is laid over damaged skin

hormone chemical message produced by cells and transported in the blood to target cells where the message brings about an effect

human immunodeficiency virus (HIV) the virus that causes acquired immune deficiency syndrome (AIDS) in humans

insulin hormone that controls the levels of glucose in the blood. A lack of insulin causes diabetes.

laser instrument that generates an intense beam of light of a specific wavelength. Used in surgery to cut open tissue or remove blemishes.

liposuction the removal of fat from the body using a suction technique

magnetic resonance imaging (MRI) scanner machine that uses a strong magnetic field to generate images of the inside of the body

microsurgery delicate surgery carried out on tissues, blood vessels and nerves using a microscope and very fine instruments

optical fibres thin glass fibres through which light can be transmitted

paralyse/paralysis condition in which impulses do not travel along nerves, preventing muscles from working

polymers compound made of one or more large molecules that are formed from repeated units of smaller molecules

protein large organic molecule made up of chains of amino acids

puberty period in a girl or boy's development when their bodies begin to change as they become adults

rejection when the body's defence (immune) system reacts against a transplanted tissue or organ so that it does not survive

rhinoplasty procedure to reshape the nose

rhytidectomy complete facelift

scalpel sharp blade used by surgeons

selective breeding the careful selection of individuals with certain characteristics to be the parents of the next generation. In time, the appearance of the species or variety changes; for example the breeding of plants with a particular shape or colour of flower, or the characteristics of a certain breed of dog.

Silicon Valley area in California where a large number of hi-tech industries are located

silicone substance produced when silicon is combined with oxygen, carbon and hydrogen. It can be liquid or solid and is relatively inert so can be used in implants which are inserted into the body.

stem cells cells that have the ability to grow into a number of different types of specialist cells

sutures stitches used to close a wound

synthetic artificial, made by a chemical process

testes parts of the male sex organ where sperm is produced

testosterone steroid hormone, produced in the testes, which is involved in the production of sperm and is responsible for male sexual characteristics

tissue group of cells of the same type which act together to carry out a particular role; for example, liver tissue and epidermal tissue

transplant when living tissues and implants are removed in another part of the body, or in another body

virtual reality not physically existing but made by software to appear to do so

wavelength distance between two successive peaks or troughs of a wave. The shorter the distance, the shorter the wavelength.

Sources of information

Further reading

Science at the Edge: Cloning, Sally Morgan
  (Heinemann Library 2002)
Science at the Edge: Frontiers of Surgery, Ann Fullick
  (Heinemann Library 2005)

Many magazines such as *New Scientist*, *Biological Review*, *Focus* and *Science* and newspapers such as *The Guardian* write about plastic surgery in an accessible manner.

Websites

A number of websites have up-to-date information on plastic surgery:

http://www.bbc.co.uk
The BBC has produced a number of programmes on the face, the human body and reconstructive surgery and genetic disorders. Each programme has a comprehensive website giving more details.

http://www.surgery.org/index.asp
The American Society for Aesthetic Plastic Surgery (ASAPS) is the leading organization of plastic surgeons specializing in cosmetic plastic surgery. The website provides unbiased information on the whole range of cosmetic techniques.

www.savingfaces.co.uk
The Facial Surgery Research Foundation is a charity that researches into the prevention and treatment of oral and facial diseases and injuries.

Author sources

The following sources were also used by the author in the writing of this book:

Advanced Biology Principles and Applications, CJ Clegg and DG Mackean (John Murray, 2000)

A variety of websites about cosmetic and reconstructive surgery.

Index